Be An Expert!™

What Is the Weather?

Erin Kelly

Children's Press®

An imprint of Scholastic Inc.

Contents

It Is Sunny 4

It Is Cloudy 6

Know the Names

Be an expert! Get to know the names of these kinds of weather.

It Is Windy 12

A Rainbow! 18

It Is Raining 8

It Is Snowing 10

I See Lightning 14

BOOM!

I Hear Thunder 16

BOOM!

All the Weather 20

Expert Quiz 21

Expert Gear 22

Glossary............................... 23

Index..................................... 24

3

It Is Sunny

The sun shines in the sky.
It is a beautiful day!

Zoom In

Find these objects in the big picture.

sunglasses **beach ball** **sunscreen** **sunflower**

It Is Cloudy

Clouds fill the sky.
They hide the sun.

Be Prepared

Q: What is a cloud made of?

A: A cloud is made up of tiny **water droplets**.

It Is Raining

Water falls from the sky.
Grab your umbrella!

When the water droplets in a cloud get big and heavy, they fall as rain.

9

It Is Snowing

Snow is falling.
It is cold today. Brr!

Be Prepared

Q: How do snowflakes form?

A: When the air gets cold, water droplets **freeze**. Snowflakes form as a lot of droplets freeze together.

It Is Windy

WHOOSH.

You can feel the air moving.

Wind can be gentle or strong.

Expert Fact

A **wind sock** can tell you in which direction the wind is blowing.

I See Lightning

FLASH!

The sky is lit up.

Be Prepared

Q: What do I do if I see lightning?

A: Go indoors. If you can't, stay away from trees. Lightning often **strikes** the tallest things in the area.

I Hear Thunder

BOOM!

Thunder is loud.

Expert Fact

Thunder is the sound lightning makes when it moves through the air.

BOOM!

17

A Rainbow!

Pretty colors appear in the sky.
Can you name them all?

Be Prepared

Q: How is a rainbow formed?

A: A rainbow appears when the sun shines through water droplets in the air.

All the Weather

So many types of weather.
What is the weather today?

1.

2.

5.

6.

Expert Quiz

Do you know the names of these kinds of weather events? Then you are an expert! See if someone else can name them too!

3.

BOOM!

4.

7.

8.

Answers: 1. Cloudy 2. Rainbow 3. Thunder 4. Raining 5. Lightning 6. Sunny 7. Snowing 8. Windy.

21

Expert Gear

Meet a storm tracker. What gear does she need to study a storm?

She has a **flashlight**.

She has **radar**.

She has a **truck**.

She has a **raincoat**.

She has a **camera**.

Glossary

freeze (FREEZ): to become solid or turn into ice at a very low temperature.

strikes (STRIKES): hits or attacks suddenly. Lightning sometimes strikes tall trees.

water droplets (WAW-tuhr DROP-letz): tiny drops of water.

wind sock (WIND SAHK): a large fabric tube that is placed on a pole and used to show the direction of the wind.

Index

beach ball.................. 5

clouds/cloudy...6–7, 9

cold 10, 11

flashlight.................22

freeze.................11, 23

lightning.............14–15, 16, 23

radar 22

rain/raining..........8–9

rainbow 18–19

raincoat...................22

snow/snowing....10–11

snowflakes 11

storm tracker 22

strikes 14, 23

sun/sunny............ 4–5, 6, 19

sunflower 5

sunglasses................ 5

sunscreen 5

thunder 16–17

truck 22

umbrella................... 8

water 7, 8, 9, 11, 19, 23

wind 12–13, 23

Library of Congress Cataloging-in-Publication Data
Names: Kelly, Erin Suzanne, 1965– author.
Title: What is the weather?/by Erin Kelly.
Other titles: Be an expert! (Scholastic Inc.)
Description: Book edition. | New York: Children's Press, an imprint of Scholastic Inc., 2022. | Series: Be an expert | Includes index. | Audience: Ages 3–5. | Audience: Grades K–1. | Summary: "Some days it is sunny. Some days it is cloudy. Sometimes we even see a rainbow! What do you know about the weather? With this book, you can become an expert! Feel like a pro with exciting photos, expert facts, and fun challenges. Can you name which days are rainy and which are snowy? Try it! Then see if you can pass the Expert Quiz!"—Provided by publisher.
Identifiers: LCCN 2021025486 (print) | LCCN 2021025487 (ebook) | ISBN 9781338797930 (library binding) | ISBN 9781338797947 (paperback) | ISBN 9781338797954 (ebk)
Subjects: LCSH: Weather—Juvenile literature. | Meteorology—Juvenile literature.
Classification: LCC QC981.3.K458 2022 (print) | LCC QC981.3 (ebook) | DDC 551.5—dc23
LC record available at https://lccn.loc.gov/2021025486
LC ebook record available at https://lccn.loc.gov/2021025487

10 9 8 7 6 5 4 3 2 1   22 23 24 25 26

Printed in Heshan, China 62
First edition, 2022

Series produced by Spooky Cheetah Press
Design by The Design Lab, Kathleen Petelinsek

Photos ©: 7 inset top: Kemter/Getty Images; 9 inset: Photobug44/Dreamstime; 10 left: Jarenwicklund/Dreamstime; 12 left: Tom Merton/Getty Images; 13 inset left: Tetra Images/PT Images/Getty Images; 22: Ryan McGinnis/Alamy Images; 23 center top: Pascal Halder/Dreamstime; 23 bottom: Ivonne Wierink/Dreamstime.

All other photos © Shutterstock.